THE PIRATES

OF

PENZANCE

AUTHORIZED COPYRIGHT EDITION

THE PIRATES

OF

PENZANCE

OR

The Slave of Duty

COMIC OPERA

BY

W. S. GILBERT AND ARTHUR SULLIVAN,
A uthors of "Pinafore,"etc,etc

IN TWO ACTS

COMPLETE LIBRETTO

KALPAZ

ISBN: 978-93-5128-572-4

First Published in 1880
Indian Reprint in 2017

Published by

Kalpaz Publications
C-30, Satyawati Nagar,
Delhi – 110052
E-mail: kalpaz@hotmail.com
Website: kalpazpublications.com
Ph.: +91-9212142040

Cataloging in Publication Data—DK
Courtesy: D.K. Agencies (P) Ltd. <docinfo@dkagencies.com>

Sullivan, Arthur, 1842-1900, **composer.**
[Pirates of Penzance. Libretto]
The pirates of Penzance, or, The slave of duty : comic opera : in two acts, complete libretto / written by W.S. Gilbert ; and composed by Arthur Sullivan. — Authorized copyright edition.
pages cm
"First published in 1880"—Title page verso.
ISBN 9789351285724

1. Operas—Librettos. I. Gilbert, W. S. (William Schwenck), 1836-1911, librettist. II. Title. III. Title: Slave of duty.

ML50.S96P5 2017 DDC 782.120268 23

THE BOSTON IDEAL OPERA COMPANY.

E. H. OBER, Manager.

THE PIRATES OF PENZANCE

OR,

THE SLAVE OF DUTY.

Written by W. S. GILBERT. **Composed by ARTHUR SULLIVAN.**

DRAMATIS PERSONÆ.

RICHARD, a Pirate Chief . . . . Mr. M. W. WHITNEY.

SAMUEL, his Lieutenant . . . . Mr. W. H. MACDONALD.

FREDERIC, a Pirate Apprentice . . . . Mr. TOM KARL. OR Mr. W. H. FESSENDEN.

MAJOR-GENERAL STANLEY, of the British army . Mr. H. C. BARNABEE.

EDWARD, a Sergeant of Police . . . . Mr. GEO. FROTHINGHAM.

MABEL, General Stanley's Youngest Daughter . Miss MARIE STONE.

KATE, EDITH, ISABEL, General Stanley's Daughters . . Miss LIZZIE BURTON. Miss H. A. BROWN. Miss MAY CALEF.

RUTH, a Piratical "Maid-of-all-work" . . . . . Miss ADELAIDE PHILLIPPS.

General Stanley's Daughters, Pirates, Policemen, etc.

SCENE.

ACT. 1ST.—*A Rocky Seashore on the Coast of Cornwall, England.*

ACT 2D.—*A Ruined Chapel on General Stanley's Estate.*

THE PIRATES OF PENZANCE;

OR,

THE SLAVE OF DUTY.

SCENE.—*A rocky sea-shore on the coast of Cornwall. Rocks L., sloping down to L. C. of stage. Under these rocks is a cavern, the entrance to which is seen at first entrance L. A natural arch of rock occupies the R. C. of the stage. In the distance is a calm sea, on which a schooner is lying at anchor.*

As the curtain rises groups of Pirates are discovered, some drinking, some playing cards. SAMUEL, *the Pirate Lieutenant, is going from one group to another, filling the cups from a flask.* FREDERIC *is seated in a despondent attitude at the back of the scene, C.* RUTH *kneels at his feet.*

OPENING CHORUS.

Pour, oh pour the pirate sherry!
  Fill, oh fill the pirate glass!
And, to make us more than merry,
  Let the pirate bumper pass.

SOLO.—SAMUEL.

For to-day our pirate 'prentice
  Rises from indentures freed.
Strong his arm and keen his scent is;
  He's a pirate now indeed!

ALL.

Here's good luck to Frederic's ventures!
Frederic's out of his indentures!

SOLO.—SAMUEL.

Two-and-twenty, now he's rising,
  And alone he's fit to fly;
Which we're bent on signalizing
  With unusual revelry.

ALL.

Here's good luck to Frederic's ventures!
Frederic's out of his indentures!
  So pour, oh pour the pirate sherry, etc.

(FREDERIC *rises and comes forward with Pirate King, who enters from R. U. E.*)

KING. Yes, Frederic, from to-day you rank as a full-blown member of our band.

ALL. Hurrah!

FREDERIC. My friends, I thank you all, from my heart, for your kindly wishes. Would that I could repay them as they deserve!

KING. What do you mean?

FRED. To-day I am out of my indentures, and to-day I leave you for ever.

ALL. Leave us?

FRED. For ever!

KING. But this is quite unaccountable. A keener hand at scuttling a Cunarder or cutting out a White Star never shipped a handspike.

FRED. Yes, I have done my best for you. And why? It was my duty under my indentures, and I am the slave of duty. As a child I was regularly apprenticed to your band. It was through an error. No matter, the mistake was ours, not yours, and I was in honor bound by it.

SAMUEL. An error? What error?

FRED. I may not tell you. It would reflect upon my well-loved Ruth.

(RUTH *comes down C.*)

RUTH. Nay, dear master, my mind has long been gnawed by the cankering tooth of mystery. Better have it out at once.

SONG.—RUTH.

When Frederic was a little lad he proved so brave and daring
His father thought he'd 'prentice him to some career seafaring.
I was, alas! his nursery-maid, and so it fell to *my* lot
To take and bind this promising boy apprentice to a pilot.
A life not bad for a hardy lad, though certainly not a high lot;
Though I'm a nurse, you might do worse than make your boy a pilot.

I was a stupid nursery-maid, on breakers always steering,
And I did not catch the word aright, through being hard of hearing.
Mistaking my instructions, which within my brain did *gyrate*,
I took and bound this promising boy apprentice to a pirate.
A sad mistake it was to make, and doom him to a vile lot:
I bound him to a pirate—you—instead of to a pilot!

I soon found out, beyond all doubt, the scope of this disaster;
But I hadn't the face to return to my place and break it to my master.
A nursery-maid is never afraid of what you people *call* work,
So I made up my mind to go as a kind of piratical maid-of-all-work;
And that is how you find me now a member of your shy lot,
Which you wouldn't have found had he been bound apprentice to a pilot.

RUTH. (*Kneeling at his feet.*) Oh pardon, Frederic! pardon!

FRED. Rise, sweet one; I have long pardoned you. (RUTH *rises.*)

RUTH. The two words were so much alike!

FRED. They still are, though years have rolled over their heads! (RUTH *goes up with* SAMUEL.) But this afternoon my obligation ceases. Individually, I love you all with affection unspeakable; but collectively, I look upon you with a disgust that amounts to absolute detestation. Oh pity me, my beloved friends, for such is my sense of duty that once out of my indentures I shall feel myself bound to devote myself, heart and soul, to your extermination.

ALL. Poor lad! poor lad! (*All weep.*)

KING. Well, Frederic, if you conscientiously feel that it is your duty to destroy us, we cannot blame you for acting on that conviction. Always act in accordance with the dictates of your conscience, my boy, and chance the consequences.

SAMUEL. Besides, we can offer you but little temptation to remain with us. We don't seem to make piracy pay. I'm sure I don't know why, but we don't.

FRED. I know why, but, alas! I mustn't tell you: it wouldn't be right.

KING. Why not, my boy? It's only half-past eleven, and you are one of us until the clock strikes twelve.

SAM. True, and until then you are bound to protect our interests.

ALL. Hear! hear!

FRED. Well, then, it is my duty as a pirate to tell you that you are too tender-hearted. For instance, you make a point of never attacking a weaker party than yourselves, and when you attack a stronger party you invariably get thrashed.

KING. There is some truth in that.

FRED. Then, again, you make a point of never molesting an orphan.

SAM. Of course: we are orphans ourselves, and know what it is.

FRED. Yes, but it has got about, and what is the consequence? Every one we capture says he's an orphan. The last three ships we took proved to be manned entirely by orphans, and so we had to let 'em go. One would think that Great Britain's mercantile navy was recruited solely from her orphan asylums, which we know is not the case. (*Crosses R.*)

SAM. But, hang it all! you wouldn't have us absolutely merciless?

FRED. There's my difficulty. Until twelve o'clock I would; after twelve o'clock I wouldn't. Was ever a man placed in so delicate a situation?

(RUTH *comes down C.*)

RUTH. And Ruth, your own Ruth, whom you love so well, and who has won her middle-aged way into your boyish heart—what is to become of her?

KING. Oh, he will take you with him.

FRED. Well, Ruth, I feel some little difficulty about you. It is true that I admire you very much, but I have been constantly at sea since I was eight years old, and yours is the only woman's face I have seen during that time. I think it is a sweet face.

RUTH. It is—oh, it is!

FRED. I say I *think* it is—that is my impression. But as I have never had an opportunity of comparing you with other women, it is just possible I may be mistaken.

KING. True.

FRED. What a terrible thing it would be if I were to marry this innocent person, and then find out that she is, on the whole, plain!

KING. Oh, Ruth is very well—very well indeed.

SAM. Yes, there are the remains of a fine woman about Ruth.

FRED. Do you really think so? Then I will not be so selfish as to take her from you. In justice to her and in consideration for you I will leave her behind. (*Hands* RUTH *to* KING.)

KING. No, Frederic, this must not be. We are rough men, who lead a rough life, but we are not so utterly heartless as to deprive thee of thy love. I think I am right in saying that there is not one here who would deprive thee of this inestimable treasure for all the world holds dear.

ALL. (*Loudly.*) Not one!

KING. No, I thought there wasn't. Keep thy love, Frederic—keep thy love! (*Hands her back to* FREDERIC.)

FRED. You're very good, I'm sure.

KING. Well, it's the top of the tide, and we must be off. Farewell, Frederic. When your process of extermination begins, let our deaths be as swift and painless as you can conveniently make them.

FRED. I will. By the love I have for you, I swear it. Would that you could render this extermination unnecessary by accompanying me back to civilization!

KING. No, Frederic, it cannot be. I don't think much of our profession, but, contrasted with respectability, it is comparatively honest. No, Frederic; I shall live and die a pirate king.

SONG.—PIRATE KING.

Oh better far to live and die
Under the brave black flag I fly,
Than play a sanctimonious part
With a pirate head and a pirate heart.
Away to the cheating world go you,
Where pirates all are well-to-do;
But I'll be true to the song I sing,
And live and die a Pirate King!
For I am a Pirate King!

ALL. You are! Hurrah for the Pirate King!

KING. And it is, it is a glorious thing
To be a Pirate King!

ALL. It is! Hurrah for our Pirate King!

KING. When I sally forth to seek my prey
I help myself in a royal way.
I sink a few more ships, it's true,
Than a well-bred monarch ought to do;
But many a king on a first-class throne,
If he wants to call his crown his own,
Must manage somehow to get through
More dirty work than ever *I* do,
Though I am a Pirate King.

ALL. You are! Hurrah for the Pirate King!

KING. And it is, it is a glorious thing
To be a Pirate King!

ALL. It is! Hurrah for our Pirate King!

(*After Song, the* KING, SAMUEL, *and all the Pirates, except* FREDERIC *and* RUTH, *go off R. and R. U. E.* FREDERIC *comes down C., followed by* RUTH.)

RUTH. Oh take me with you! I cannot live if I am left behind.

FRED. Ruth, I will be quite candid with you. You are very dear to me, as you know, but I must be circumspect. You see, you are considerably older than I: a lad of twenty-one usually looks for a wife of seventeen.

RUTH. A wife of seventeen! You will find me a wife of a thousand!

FRED. No, but I shall find you a wife of forty-seven, and that is quite enough now. Ruth, tell me candidly and without reserve: compared with other women, how are *you?*

RUTH. I will answer you truthfully, master: I have a slight cold, but otherwise I am quite well.

FRED. I am sorry for your cold, but I was referring rather to your personal appearance. Compared with other women, are you beautiful?

RUTH. (*Bashfully.*) I have been told so, dear master.

FRED. Ah, but lately?

RUTH. Oh no; years and years ago.

FRED. But what do you think yourself?

RUTH. It is a delicate question to answer, but I think I am a fine woman.

FRED. That is your candid opinion?

RUTH. Yes: I should be deceiving you if I told you otherwise.

FRED. Thank you, Ruth, I believe you, for I am sure you would not practise on my inexperience. I wish to do the right thing, and if—I say, *if*—you are really a fine woman, your age shall be no obstacle to our union. (*Shakes hands with her.*)

(*Chorus of girls heard in the extreme distance, "Climbing over rocky mountains," etc. See entrance of girls.*)

FRED. Hark! surely I hear voices. Who has ventured to approach our all but inaccessible lair? Can it be custom-house? No, it does not sound like custom-house.

RUTH. (*Aside.*) Confusion! It is the voices of young girls! If he should see them I am lost.

FRED. (*Climbing rocky arch R. C. and looking off L.*) By all that's marvellous, a bevy of beautiful maidens!

RUTH. (*Aside.*) Lost! lost! lost!

FRED. How lovely, how surpassingly lovely, is the plainest of them! What grace! what delicacy! what refinement! and Ruth—Ruth told me she was beautiful!

RECIT.

FRED. Oh false one, you have deceived me!

RUTH. I have deceived you?

FRED. Yes, deceived me! (*Denouncing her.*)

DUET—FREDERIC *and* RUTH.

FRED. You told me you were fair as gold.
RUTH. (*Wildly.*) And, master, am I not so?
FRED. And now I see you're plain and old.
RUTH. I am sure I am not a jot so.
FRED. Upon my innocence you play.
RUTH. I'm not the one to plot so.
FRED. Your face is lined, your hair is gray.
RUTH. It's gradually got so.
FRED. Faithless woman, to deceive me!—I who trusted so!
RUTH. Master, master, do not leave me; hear me ere you go!

My love, without reflecting,
Oh do not be rejecting.
Take a maiden tender, her affection raw and green,
At very highest rating
Has been accumulating
Summers seventeen, summers seventeen.

Don't, beloved master,
Crush me with disaster!
What is such a dower to the dower I have here?
My love, unabating,
Has been accumulating
Forty-seven year, forty-seven year!

ENSEMBLE.

RUTH.

Don't, beloved master,
Crush me with disaster, etc.
What is such a dower to the dower I have here? etc.

FRED.

Yes, your former master
Saves you from disaster.
Your love would be uncomfortably fervid, it is clear,
If, as you are stating,
It's been accumulating
Forty-seven year, forty-seven year!

(*At the end he renounces her, and she goes off R. in despair.*)

RECIT.—FRED.

What shall I do? Before these gentle maidens I dare not show in this alarming costume. No, no, I must remain in close concealment until I can appear in decent clothing. (*Exit R.*)

(*Hides in cave as they enter from R. and L., climbing over the rocks at L. of the stage and through arched rock R.*)

FRED.

Climbing over rocky mountain,
Skipping rivulet and fountain,

Passing where the willows quiver
By the ever-rolling river,
  Swollen with the summer rain;
Threading long and leafy mazes,
Dotted with unnumbered daisies,
Scaling rough and rugged passes,
Climb the hardy little lasses,
  Till the bright seashore they gain.

EDITH.

Let us gayly tread the measure,
Make the most of fleeting pleasure,
Hail it as a true ally,
Though it perish by and by.

ALL.

Hail it as a true ally,
Though it perish by and by.

EDITH.

Every moment brings a treasure
Of its own especial pleasure:
Though the moments quickly die,
Greet them gayly as they fly. *(Dance.)*

KATE.

Far away from toil and care,
Revelling in fresh sea-air,
Here we live and reign alone,
In a world that's all our own.

Here, in this our rocky den,
Far away from mortal men,
We'll be queens and make decrees:
They may honor them who please.

ALL.

Let us gayly tread the measure, etc.

KATE. What a picturesque spot! I wonder where we are?

EDITH. And I wonder where papa is? We have left him ever so far behind.

ISABEL. Oh, he will be here presently. Remember, poor papa is not as young as we are, and we came over a rather difficult country.

KATE. But how thoroughly delightful it is to be so entirely alone! Why, in all probability we are the first human beings who ever set foot on this enchanting spot.

ISABEL. Except the mermaids: it's the very place for mermaids—

KATE. Who are only human beings down to the waist—

EDITH. And who can't be said, strictly, to set *foot* anywhere. Tails they may, but feet they *cannot.*

KATE. But what shall we do until papa and the servants arrive with the luncheon? (*All listen and come down.*)

EDITH. We are quite alone, and the sea is as smooth as glass. Suppose we take off our shoes and stockings and paddle?

ALL. Yes, yes—the very thing!

(*They prepare to carry out the suggestion. They have all taken off one shoe, when* FREDERIC *comes forward from cave.*)

FRED. (*Recitative.*) Stop, ladies, pray!

ALL. (*Hopping on one foot.*) A man!

FRED. I had intended
Not to intrude myself upon your notice
In this effective but alarming costume,
But under these peculiar circumstances it is my bounden duty to inform you
That your proceedings will not be unwitnessed.

EDITH. But who are you, sir? Speak! (*All hopping.*)

FRED. I am a pirate!

ALL. (*Recoiling, hopping.*) A pirate! Horror!

FRED. Ladies, do not shun me.
This evening I renounce my vile profession,
And to that end, O pure and peerless maidens,
O blushing buds of ever-blooming beauty,
I, sore of heart, implore your kind assistance.

EDITH. How pitiful his tale!

KATE. How rare his beauty!

ALL. How pitiful his tale! how rare his beauty! (*Put on their shoes.*)

SONG.—FREDERIC.

Oh is there not one maiden breast
  Which does not feel the moral beauty
Of making worldly interest
  Subordinate to sense of duty?
Who would not give up willingly
  All matrimonial ambition
To rescue such an one as I
  From his unfortunate position? (*Crosses R.*)

ALL. Alas! there's not one maiden breast
  Which seems to feel the moral beauty
Of making worldly interest
  Subordinate to sense of duty.

FRED.

Oh, is there not one maiden here
   Whose homely face and bad complexion
Have caused all hope to disappear
   Of ever winning man's affection?
To such an one, if such there be,
   I swear, by heaven's arch above you,
If you will cast your eyes on me,
   However plain you be, I'll love you.

ALL.

Alas! there's not one maiden here
   Whose homely face and bad complexion
Have caused all hope to disappear
   Of ever winning man's affection.

FRED. (*In despair.*) Not one?
ALL. No, no, not one.
FRED. Not one?
ALL. No, no!

(MABEL *enters through arch R. C.*).

MABEL. Yes, one!
ALL. 'Tis Mabel!
MABEL. Yes, 'tis Mabel!

RECIT.—MABEL.

O sisters, deaf to pity's name?
      For shame!
It's true that he has gone astray,
      But, pray,
Is that a reason good and true
      Why you
Should all be deaf to pity's name?
      For shame!

ALL. (*Aside.*) The question is, had he not been
      A thing of beauty,
Would she be swayed by quite as keen
      A sense of duty?

SOLO.—MABEL.

Poor wandering one,
   Though thou hast surely strayed,
Take heart of grace;
Thy steps retrace;
   Be not afraid.

Poor wandering one,.
If such poor love as mine
Can help thee find
True peace of mind,
Why, take it—it is thine.

ALL. Take heart! no danger lowers;
Take any heart—but ours!

MABEL. Take heart! fair days will shine.
Take any heart—take mine!

(MABEL *and* FRED *exit L.*)

(MABEL *and* FRED *go to mouth of cave L., and converse.* KATE *beckons her sisters, who form in a semicircle around her.*)

EDITH.

What ought we to do,
  Gentle sisters, say?
Propriety, we know,
  Says we ought to stay,
While sympathy exclaims,
  "Free them from your tether;
Play at other games;
  Leave them here together."

KATE.

Her case may any day
  Be yours, my dear, or mine;
Let her make her hay
  While the sun doth shine.
Let us compromise
  (Our hearts are not of leather):
Let us shut our eyes
  And talk about the weather.

(EDITH, KATE, *and girls retire up, and sit two and two, facing each other, in a line across the stage.*)

(CHATTERING CHORUS, *during which* FRED *and* MABEL *fondle.*)

How beautifully blue the sky!
The glass is rising very high.
Continue fine I hope it may,
And yet it rained but yesterday:
To-morrow it may pour again
(I hear the country wants some rain);
Yet people say, I know not why,
That we shall have a warm July.

SOLO.—MABEL.

(*During this the girls continue their chatter* pianissimo, *but listening eagerly all the time.*)

Did ever maiden wake
  From dream of homely duty
To find her daylight break
  With such exceeding beauty?
Did ever maiden close
  Her eyes on wakening sadness,
To dream of, Goodness knows,
  How much exceeding gladness?

FRED.

Ah yes, ah yes, this is exceeding gladness.

(FREDERIC *and* MABEL *turn and see that the girls are listening; detected, they continue their chatter*, forte.)

GIRLS.

How beautifully blue the sky! etc. etc.

SOLO—FRED.

(*During this the girls continue their chatter*, pianissimo, *as before, but listening intently all the time.*)

Did ever pirate roll
  His soul in guilty dreaming,
And wake to find that soul
  With peace and virtue beaming?
Did ever pirate loathed
  Forsake his hideous mission,
To find himself betrothed
  To a lady of position?

MABEL.

Ah yes, ah yes, I am a lady of position.

(MABEL *and* FRED *turn as before. Girls resume their chatter*, forte.)

ENSEMBLE.

MABEL.	FRED.	GIRLS.
Did ever maiden wake, etc.	Did ever pirate loathed, etc.	How beautifully blue the sky, etc.

REC.—FRED.

Stay; we must not lose our senses
Men who stick at no offences
  Will anon be here.

Piracy their dreadful trade is;
Pray you get you hence, young ladies,
While the coast is clear.

GIRLS.

No, we must not lose our senses,
If they stick at no offences.
We should not be here.
Piracy their dreadful trade is—
Nice companions for young ladies!
Let us disappear.

(*During this Chorus the Pirates enter stealthily from R. U. E., and form in a semicircle behind the girls. As the girls move to go off, each Pirate seizes a girl.*)

ALL. Too late!
PIRATES. Ha! ha!
ALL. Too late!
Ha! ha!

PIRATES.

Ha! ha! ha! ha! ho! ho! ho! ho!

ENSEMBLE.

PIRATES.

Now here's a first-rate opportunity
To get married with impunity,
And indulge in the felicity
Of unbounded domesticity.
You shall quickly be parsonified,
Conjugally matrimonified,
By a doctor of divinity
Who is located in this vicinity.

LADIES.

We have missed our opportunity
Of escaping with impunity;
So farewell to the felicity
Of our maiden domesticity.
We shall quickly be parsonified,
Conjugally matrimonified,
By a doctor of divinity
Who is located in this vicinity.

MABEL (*coming forward*), RECIT.

Hold, monsters! ere your pirate caravanserai
Proceeds against our will to wed us all,
Just bear in mind that we are wards in chancery,
And father is a Major-General!

SAMUEL.

We'd better pause, or dangers may befall;
Their father is a Major-General.

ALL THE LADIES.

Yes, yes, he is a Major-General.

(*The Major-General has entered unnoticed on rock L. U. E.*)

GENERAL. Yes, I am a Major-General!
ALL. You are! Hurrah for the Major-General!
GENERAL. And it is a glorious thing to be a Major-General!
ALL. It is! Hurrah for the Major-General!

SONG—MAJOR GENERAL.

I am the very pattern of a modern major-gineral:
I've information vegetable, animal, and mineral;
I know the kings of England, and I quote the fights historical,
From Marathon to Waterloo, in order categorical;
I'm very well acquainted, too, with matters mathematical;
I understand equations, both the simple and quadratical;
About binomial theorem I'm teeming with a lot of news—
(*Bothered for next rhyme.*) Lot o' news—lot o' news—
(*Struck with an idea.*) With many cheerful facts about the square of the hypotenuse;
(*Joyfully.*) With many cheerful facts about the square of the hypotenuse!

ALL.

With many cheerful facts about the square of the hypotenuse!

GENERAL.

I'm very good at integral and differential calculus;
I know the scientific names of beings animalculous;
In short, in matters vegetable, animal, and mineral
I am the very model of a modern major-gineral!

ALL.

In short in matters vegetable, animal, and mineral
He is the very model of a modern major-gineral!

GENERAL.

I know our mythic history, King Arthur's and Sir Caradoc's;
I answer hard acrostics; I've a pretty taste for paradox—
I quote in elegiacs all the crimes of Heliogabalus;
In conics I can floor peculiarities parabolous;
I can tell undoubted Raphaels from Gerard Dows and Zoffanies;
I know the croaking chorus from the "*Frogs* of Aristophanes;"
Then I can hum a fugue of which I've heard the music's din afore—
(*Bothered for next rhyme.*) Din afore? din afore? din afore?—
(*Struck with an idea.*) And whistle all the airs from that infernal nonsense, *Pinafore*,
(*Joyously.*) And whistle all the airs from that infernal nonsense, *Pinafore.*

ALL.

And whistle all the airs from that infernal nonsense, *Pinafore.*

GENERAL.

Then I can write a washing-bill in Babylonic cuneiform,
And tell you every detail of Caractacus's uniform.
In short, in matters vegetable, animal, and mineral
I am the very model of a modern major-gineral!

ALL.

In short, in matters vegetable, animal, and mineral
He is the very pattern of a modern major-gineral!

GENERAL.

In fact, when I know what is meant by "mamelon" and "ravelin"—
When I can tell at sight a chassepot rifle from a javelin—
When such affairs as sorties and surprises I'm more wary at,
And when I know precisely what is meant by "commissariat"—
When I have learnt what progress has been made in modern gunnery—
When I know more of tactics than a novice in a nunnery,—
In short, when I've a smattering of elemental strategy—
(*Bothered for the rhyme.*) Strategy! strategy!—
(*Struck with an idea.*)
(*Joyously.*) You'll say a better major-general has never *sat* agee.

ALL.

We'll say a better major-general has never *sat* agee.

GENERAL.

For my military knowledge, though I'm plucky and adventury,
Has only been brought down to the beginning of the century;
But still, in matters vegetable, animal, and mineral
I am the very model of a modern major-gineral.

ALL.

But still in learning vegetable, animal, and mineral
He is the very model of a modern major-gineral.

GENERAL. And now that I've introduced myself, I should like to have some idea of what's going on.

KATE. Oh, papa! we—

SAMUEL. Permit me; I'll explain it in two words: we propose to marry your daughters.

GENERAL. Dear me!

GIRLS. Against our wills, papa—against our wills!

GENERAL. Oh, but you mustn't do that. May I ask—this is a picturesque uniform, but I'm not familiar with it—what are you?

KING. We are all single gentlemen.

GENERAL. Yes, I gathered that. Anything else?

KING. No, nothing else.

EDITH. Papa, don't believe them. They are pirates—the famous Pirates of Penzance!

GENERAL. The Pirates of Penzance? I have often heard of them.

MABEL. Yes, all except this gentleman (*indicating* FREDERIC), who was a pirate once, but who is out of his indentures to-day.

GENERAL. But wait a bit. I object to pirates as sons-in-law.

KING. We object to major-generals as fathers-in-law. But we waive that point; we do not press it, we look over it.

GENERAL. (*Aside.*) Hah! an idea! (*Aloud.*) And do you mean to say that you would deliberately rob me of these the sole remaining props of my old age, and leave me to go through the remainder of life unfriended, unprotected, and alone?

KING. Well, yes; that's the idea.

GENERAL. Tell me, have you ever known what it is to be an orphan?

ALL THE PIRATES. (*Disgusted.*) Oh, dash it all!

KING. Here we are again!

GENERAL. I ask you, Have you ever known what it is to be an orphan?

KING. (*Sighing.*) Often.

GENERAL. Yes, orphan. Have you ever known what it is to be one?

KING. I say, often.

ALL. (*Disgusted.*) Often! often! often! (*Turning away.*)

GENERAL. I don't think we quite understand one another. I ask you, Have you ever known what it is to be an orphan? and you say "Orphan." As I understand you, you are merely repeating the word "orphan" to show that you understand me.

KING. I didn't repeat the word "often."

GENERAL. Pardon me; you did indeed.

KING. I only repeated it once.

GENERAL. True, but you repeated it.

KING. But not often.

GENERAL. Stop! I think I see where we are getting confused. When you said "orphan" did you mean "orphan," a person who has lost his parents, or "often," frequently?

KING. Oh, I beg your pardon! I see you mean frequently.

GENERAL. Ah, you said "often" frequently.
KING. No, only once.
GENERAL. Exactly, you said "often, frequently," only once.

FINALE.

RECIT.—GENERAL.

Oh, men of dark and dismal fate,
Forego your cruel employ;
Have pity on my lonely state—
I am an orphan boy!
KING. An orphan boy?
GENERAL. An orphan boy!
PIRATES. How sad! an orphan boy!

SOLO.—GENERAL.

These children whom you see
Are all that I can call my own.
PIRATES. Poor fellow!
GENERAL. Take them away from me,
And I shall be indeed alone.
PIRATES. Poor fellow!
GENERAL. If pity you can feel,
Leave me my sole remaining joy.
See, at your feet they kneel;
Your hearts you cannot steel
Against the sad, sad tale of the lonely orphan boy.
PIRATES. (*Sobbing.*) Poor fellow!
See, at our feet they kneel;
Our hearts we cannot steel
Against the sad, sad tale of the lonely orphan boy.
KING. The orphan boy!
SAM. The orphan boy!
ALL. The lonely orphan boy! Poor fellow!

ENSEMBLE.

GENERAL.

I'm telling a terrible story,
But it doesn't diminish my glory;
For they would have taken my daughters
Over the billowy waters,

GIRLS. (*Aside.*)

He's telling a terrible story,
Which will tend to diminish his glory,
Though they would have taken his daughters
Over the billowy waters.

PIRATES. (*Aside.*)

If he's telling a terrible story,
He shall die by a death that is gory—
Yes, one of the cruellest slaughters
That ever were known in these waters;

GENERAL.	GIRLS. (*Aside.*)	PIRATES. (*Aside.*)
If I hadn't in elegant diction	It's easy in elegant diction	And we'll finish his moral affliction
Indulged in an innocent fiction,	To call it an innocent fiction,	By a very complete malediction,
Which is not in the same category	But it comes in the same category	As a compliment valedictory,
As telling a regular, terrible story.	As telling a regular, terrible story.	If he's telling a regular, terrible story.

KING.

Although our dark career
  Sometimes involves the crime of stealing,
We rather think that we're
  Not altogether void of feeling.
Although we live by strife,
  We're always sorry to begin it,
For what we ask is life
  Without a touch of poetry in it.

ALL. (*Kneeling.*)

Hail, Poetry, thou heaven-born maid!
Thou gildest e'en the pirate's trade.
Hail, flowing fount of sentiment!
All hail, divine emollient!

KING.

You may go, for you're at liberty; our pirate rules protect you,
And honorary members of our band we do elect you.

SAMUEL. For he is an orphan boy!
ALL. He is! Hurrah for the orphan boy!
GENERAL. And it sometimes is a useful thing to be an orphan boy.
ALL. It is! Hurrah for the orphan boy!
Hurrah for the orphan—

MABEL, etc. Oh, happy day! with joyous glee
We will away and married be!
GENERAL. Oh, happy day! with joyous glee
They will away and married be!
MABEL. Should it befall auspiciously,
My sisters all will bridesmaids be.
GENERAL. Should it befall auspiciously,
Her sisters all will bridesmaids be.
ALL. Oh, happy day! etc.

RECIT.—RUTH.

Oh, master, hear one word, I do implore you!
Remember Ruth, your Ruth, who kneels before you!

PIRATES. Yes, yes, remember Ruth who kneels before you.
FRED. Away! you did deceive me!
PIRATES. Away! you did deceive him.
RUTH. Oh, do not leave me!
PIRATES. Oh, do not leave her!
FRED. Away! you grieve me!
PIRATES. Away! you grieve him!
FRED. I wish you'd leave me!
PIRATES. We wish you'd leave him!

ENSEMBLE.

Pray observe the magnanimity
{We / They} display to lace and dimity.
Never was such opportunity
To get married with impunity;
But {we / they} give up the felicity
Of unbounded domesticity,
Though a doctor of divinity
Is located in this vicinity.

(GIRLS *and* GENERAL *go up rocks L. Group while Pirates indulge in a wild dance of delight on stage R. and R. C. The* GENERAL *produces a British flag, and the* PIRATE KING *(on arched rock R. C.) produces a black flag with skull and crossbones. Picture.)*

END OF ACT I.

ACT II.

SCENE.—*A ruined chapel by moonlight. Aisles C., R., and L., divided by pillars and arches; ruined Gothic windows at back.* GENERAL STANLEY *discovered seated R. C. pensively, surrounded by his daughters.*

CHORUS.

Oh dry the glistening tear
  That dews that martial cheek;
Thy loving children hear,
  In them thy comfort seek.
With sympathetic care
  Their arms around thee creep,
For oh, they cannot bear
  To see their father weep.

(*Enter* MABEL *and* FRED.)

SOLO.—MABEL.

Dear father, why leave your bed
  At this untimely hour,
When happy daylight is dead
  And darksome dangers lower?
See, Heaven has lit her lamp,
  The midnight hour is past,
And the chilly night-air is damp,
  The dew is falling fast.
Dear father, why leave your bed
When happy daylight is dead?

(FRED *enters R. U. E. and down C.*)

MABEL. Oh, Frederic, cannot you reconcile it with your conscience to say something that will relieve my father's sorrow?

FRED. I will try, dear Mabel, but why does he s[illegible] after night, in this draughty old ruin?

GENERAL. Why do I sit here? To escape from the pirates' clutches I described myself as an orphan, and I am no orphan. I came here to humble myself before the tombs of my ancestors, and to implore their pardon for the disgrace I have brought upon them.

FRED. But you forget, sir. You only bought the property a year ago, and the stucco on your baronial castle is scarcely dry.

GENERAL. Frederic, in this chapel are ancestors; you cannot deny that. I don't know whose ancestors they *were*, but I know whose ancestors they *are*, and I shudder to think that their descendant by purchase (if I may so describe myself) should have brought disgrace upon what I have no doubt was an unstained escutcheon.

FRED. Be comforted. Had you not acted as you did, these reckless men would assuredly have called in the nearest clergyman, and have married your large family on the spot.

GENERAL. I thank you for your proffered solace, but it is unavailing. At what time does your expedition march against these scoundrels?

FRED. At eleven, and before midnight I hope to have atoned for my involuntary association with these pestilent scourges by sweeping them from the face of the earth.—And then, my Mabel, you will be mine!

GENERAL. Are your devoted followers at hand?

FRED. They are; they only wait my orders.

RECIT.—GENERAL. Then, Frederic, let your escort lion-hearted be summoned to receive a general's blessing ere they depart upon their dread adventure.

FRED. Dear sir, they come!

(Enter Police, marching in single file from L., 2d E., and form in line, facing audience.)

SONG.—SERGEANT.

When the foeman bares his steel—

ALL. (*Using their clubs as trumpets.*) Tarantara! tarantara!
SERGEANT. We uncomfortable feel;
ALL. Tarantara!
SERGEANT. And we find the wisest thing—
ALL. Tarantara! tarantara!
SERGEANT. Is to slap our chests and sing—
ALL. Tarantara!
SERGEANT. For when threatened with *emeutes*—
ALL. Tarantara! tarantara!
SERGEANT. And your heart is in your boots—
ALL. Tarantara!

SERGEANT. There is nothing brings it round—
ALL. Tarantara! tarantara!
SERGEANT. Like the trumpet's martial sound—
ALL. Tarantara!
SERGEANT. Tarantara-ra-ra-ra-ra-ra! etc.
ALL. Tarantara-ra-ra-ra-ra-ra!

MABEL (*from L., addressing* SERGEANT).

Go, ye heroes, go to glory!
Though you die in combat gory,
Ye shall live in song and story—
Go to immortality!
Go to death and go to slaughter;
Die, and every Cornish daughter
With her tears your graves shall water—
Go, ye heroes, go and die!
ALL. Go, ye heroes, go and die!
SERGEANT. Though to us it's evident—
ALL. Tarantara! tarantara!
SERGEANT. These attentions are well meant—
ALL. Tarantara!
SERGEANT. Such expressions don't appear—
ALL. Tarantara! tarantara!
SERGEANT. Calculated men to cheer—
ALL. Tarantara!
SERGEANT. Who are going to meet their fate—
ALL. Tarantara! tarantara!
SERGEANT. In a highly nervous state—
ALL. Tarantara!
SERGEANT. Still, to us it's evident—
ALL. Tarantara! tarantara!
SERGEANT. These attentions are well meant—
ALL. Tarantara!
ALL. Yes, to them it's evident, etc. etc.

EDITH (*from R., addressing* SERGEANT).

Go, and do your best endeavor.
And before all links we sever
We will say farewell for ever—
Go to glory and the grave!
For your foes are fierce and ruthless,
False, unmerciful, and truthless;
Young and tender, old and toothless,
All in vain their mercy crave.
ALL. Yes, your foes are fierce and ruthless, etc.

CHORUS OF POLICE.

We observe too great a stress—
Tarantara! tarantara!
On the risks that on us press—
Tarantara!
And of reference a lack—
Tarantara! tarantara!
To our chance of coming back—
Tarantara!

SERGEANT. Still, perhaps it would be wise—
POLICE. Tarantara! tarantara!
SERGEANT. Not to carp or criticise—
ALL. Tarantara!
SERGEANT. For it's very evident—
ALL. Tarantara! tarantara!
SERGEANT. These attentions are well meant—
ALL. Tarantara!
ALL. Yes, to us it's evident
These attentions are well meant—
Tarantara-ra-ra-ra-ra! etc. etc.
Go, ye heroes, go to glory! etc. etc.

GENERAL. Away! away!
POLICE. (*Without moving.*) Yes, yes, we go!
GENERAL. These pirates slay.
POLICE. Yes, yes, we go.
GENERAL. Then do not stay.
POLICE. We go, we go.
GENERAL. Then why all this delay?
POLICE. All right! We go, we go;
Yes, forward on the foe!
Ho! ho! ho! ho!
We go, we go, we go!
Tarantara-ra-ra-ra!
GENERAL. Then forward on the foe!
ALL. Yes! forward!
POLICE. Yes! forward!
GENERAL. Yes! but you *don't* go!
POLICE. We go, we go, we go!
ALL. At last they really go! Tarantara-ra-ra!

ENSEMBLE.

CHORUS OF ALL BUT POLICE.	CHORUS OF POLICE.
Go, and do your best endeavor,	Such expressions don't appear—
And before all links we sever	Tarantara! tarantara!
We will say farewell for ever;	Calculated men to cheer—
Go to glory and the grave!	Tarantara!

<table>
<tr><th>CHORUS OF ALL BUT POLICE.</th><th>CHORUS OF POLICE.</th></tr>
<tr><td>For your foes are fierce and ruthless,
False, unmerciful, and truthless;
Young and tender, old and toothless,
All in vain their mercy crave, etc.</td><td>Who are going to their fate—
Tarantara! tarantara!
In a highly nervous state—
Tarantara!
We observe too great a stress—
Tarantara! tarantara!
On the risks that on us press—
Tarantara!
And of reference a lack—
Tarantara! tarantara!
To our chance of coming back—
Tarantara!</td></tr>
</table>

(MABEL *tears herself from* FRED, *and exits R., followed by her sisters, consoling her. The* GENERAL *and others follow the Police off L.* FREDERIC *remains alone.*)

RECIT.—FRED.

Now for the pirates' lair! Oh joy unbounded!
Oh sweet relief! oh rapture unexampled!
At last I may atone, in some slight measure,
For the repeated acts of theft and pillage
Of which, at a sense of duty's stern dictation,
I, circumstances' victim, have been guilty.

(*The* PIRATE KING *and* RUTH *appear at the window C., armed.*)

KING. Young Frederic! (*Covering him with pistol.*)
FRED. Who calls?
KING. Your late commander. (*Coming down.*)
RUTH. And I, your little Ruth! (*Covering him with pistol.*)
FRED. Oh, mad intruders!
How dare ye face me? Know ye not, rash ones,
That I have doomed you to extermination?

(KING *and* RUTH *hold a pistol to each ear.*)

KING. Have mercy on us! Hear us ere you slaughter!
FRED. I do not think I ought to listen to you.
Yes, mercy should allay our stern resentment,
And so I will be merciful. Say on.

TRIO.—RUTH, KING, *and* FRED.

When first you left our pirate fold
We tried to cheer our spirits faint,
According to our customs old,
With quips and quibbles quaint;
But all in vain the quips we heard;
We lay and sobbed upon the rocks,

Until to somebody occurred
A startling paradox.

FRED. A paradox?
KING *and* RUTH. (*Laughing.*) A paradox—
A most ingenious paradox.
We've quips and quibbles heard in flocks,
But none to beat this paradox.
Ha! ha! ha! ha! Ho! ho! ho! ho!
KING. We knew your taste for curious quips,
For cranks and contradictions queer,
And with the laughter on our lips
We wished you there to hear.
We said, "If we could tell it him,
How Frederic would the joke enjoy!"
And so we've risked both life and limb
To tell it to our boy.
FRED. (*Interested.*) That paradox.
KING *and* RUTH. (*Laughing.*) That paradox,
That most ingenious paradox.
We've quips and quibbles heard in flocks,
But none to beat that paradox!
Ha! ha! ha! ha! Ho! ho! ho! ho!

CHANT.—KING.

For some ridiculous reason—to which, however, I've no desire to be disloyal—
Some person in authority—I don't know who; very likely the Astronomer-Royal—
Has decided that although for such a beastly month as February twenty-eight days as a general rule are plenty,
One year in every four his days shall be reckoned as nine-and-twenty.
Through some singular coincidence—I shouldn't be surprised if it were owing to the agency of an ill-natured fairy—
You are the victim of this clumsy arrangement, having been born in leap-year on the twenty-ninth of February;
And so, by a simple arithmetical process, you'll easily discover,
That though you've lived twenty-one years, yet, if we go by birthdays, you are only five and a little bit over!
RUTH *and* KING. Ha! ha! ha! ha! Ho! ho! ho! ho!
FRED. Dear me! Let's see: (*Counting on fingers.*)
Yes, yes,—with yours my figures do agree.
Ha! ha! ha! ha! Ho! ho! ho! ho!
(FREDERIC *more amused than any.*)

How quaint the ways of Paradox!
At common sense she gayly mocks.
Though, counting in the usual way,
  Years twenty-one I've been alive,
Yet, reckoning by my natal-day,
  I am a little boy of five!

ALL. He is a little boy of five, ha! ha!
Ha! ha! ha! ha!
KING. Ha! ha! ha! ha!
RUTH. Ha! ha! ha! ha!
FRED. Ha! ha! ha! ha!
ALL. Ha! ha! ha! ha!
  That paradox, etc.

(*All throw themselves back on seats, exhausted with laughing.*)

FRED. Upon my word, this is most curious,
Most absurdly whimsical. Five and a quarter!
No one would think it to look at me.

RUTH. You are glad now, I'll be bound, that you spared us. You would never have forgiven yourself when you discovered that you had killed two of your comrades.

FRED. My comrades?

KING. I'm afraid you don't appreciate the delicacy of your position. You were apprenticed to us—

FRED. Until I reached my twenty-first year.

KING. No, until you reached your twenty-first birthday (*producing document*), and, going by birthdays, you are as yet only five and a quarter.

FRED. You don't mean to say you are going to hold me to that?

KING. No, we merely remind you of the fact, and leave the rest to your sense of duty.

FRED. (*Wildly.*) Don't put it on that footing. As I was merciful to you just now, be merciful to me. I implore you not to insist on the letter of your bond just as the cup of happiness is at my lips.

RUTH. We insist on nothing. We content ourselves with pointing out to you your duty.

FRED. Well, you have appealed to my sense of duty, and my duty is only too clear. I abhor your infamous calling, I shudder at the thought that I have ever been mixed up with it, but duty is before all. At any cost, I will do my duty.

KING. Bravely spoken! Come, you are one of us once more.

FRED. Lead on, I follow! (*Suddenly.*) Oh, horror!

KING *and* RUTH. What is the matter?

FRED. Ought I to tell you? No! no! I cannot do it; and yet, as one of your band—

KING. Speak out, I charge you, by that sense of conscientiousness to which we have never yet appealed in vain.

FRED. General Stanley, the father of my Mabel—

KING *and* RUTH. Yes! yes!

FRED. He escaped from you on the plea that he was an orphan?

KING. He did.

FRED. It breaks my heart to betray the honored father of the girl I adore, but as your apprentice I have no alternative. It is my duty to tell you that General Stanley is no orphan.

KING *and* RUTH. What?

FRED. More than that, he never was one!

KING. Am I to understand that to save his contemptible life he dared to practise on our credulous simplicity? (FRED *nods as he weeps.*) Our revenge shall be swift and terrible. We will go and collect our band and attack Tremorden Castle this very night.

FRED. But—

KING. Not a word! he is doomed!

TRIO.

KING *and* RUTH	FRED.
Away! away! my heart's on fire; I burn, this base deception to repay; This very day my vengeance dire Shall glut itself in gore. Away! away!	Away! away! ere I expire. I find my duty hard to do to-day. My heart is filled with anguish dire; It strikes me to the core. Away! away!

KING. With falsehood foul
He tricked us of our brides;
Let vengeance howl—
The pirate so decides!
Our nature stern
He softened with his lies,
And in return
To night the traitor dies.

ALL. Yes, yes, to-night the traitor dies!

RUTH. To-night he dies.

KING. Yes, or early to-morrow.

FRED. His girls likewise?

RUTH. They will welter in sorrow!

KING. The one soft spot—

FRED. In their natures they cherish;
RUTH. And all who plot—
KING. To abuse it shall perish.
ALL. Yes, all who plot
To abuse it shall perish!
Away! away! etc.

(*Exeunt* KING *and* RUTH. FRED *throws himself on a stone L. C. in blank despair. Enter* MABEL.)

RECIT.—MABEL.

All is prepared; your gallant crew await you.
My Frederic in tears? It cannot be
That lion heart quails at the coming conflict?
FRED. No, Mabel, no. A terrible disclosure
Has just been made.
Mabel, my dearly-loved one,
I bound myself to serve the pirate captain
Until I reached my one-and-twentieth birthday.
MABEL. But you *are* twenty-one?
FRED. I've just discovered
That I was born in leap-year, and that birthday
Will not be reached by me till 1940.
MABEL. Oh horrible! catastrophe appalling!
FRED. And so farewell!
MABLE. No, no! Oh, Frederic, hear me!

DUET.—MABEL *and* FRED.

MABEL. Stay, Frederic, stay!
They have no legal claim.
No shadow of a shame
Will fall upon thy name.
Stay, Frederic, stay!
FRED. Nay, Mabel, nay!
To-night I quit these walls.
The thought my soul appalls,
But when stern duty calls
I must obey!
MABEL. Stay, Frederic, stay!
FRED. Nay, Mabel, nay!
MABEL. They have no claim.
FRED. But duty's name!
The thought my soul appalls,
But when stern duty calls
I must obey!

BALLAD.—MABEL.

Oh leave me not to pine
Alone and desolate!
No fate seemed fair as mine—
No happiness so great—
And Nature day by day
Has sung in accents clear
This joyous roundelay,
"He loves thee—he is here!
Fa la! fa la! fa la!
He loves thee—he is here!"

FRED. Oh I must leave thee here,
In endless night to dream,
Where joy is dark and drear
And sorrow all supreme—
Where nature day by day
Will sing in altered tone
This weary roundelay,
"He loves thee—he is gone!
Fa la! fa la! fa la!
He loves thee—he is gone!"
In 1940 I of age shall be:
I'll then return and claim you, I declare it!

MABEL. It seems so long!

FRED. Swear that till then you will be true to me.

MABEL. (*Aside.*) Yes, I'll be strong.
(*Aloud.*) By all the Stanleys dead and gone I swear it!

ENSEMBLE.

Oh here is love, and here is truth,
And here is food for joyous laughter:
He/She will be faithful to his/her sooth
Till we are wed, and ever after.

FRED. Farewell! Adieu!

MABEL. The same to you!

BOTH. Farewell! Adieu!

(FRED *rushes to window and leaps out.*)

RECIT.—MABEL.

(*Feeling pulse.*) Yes, I am brave! O family descent!
How great thy charm! thy sway how excellent!
Come one and all, undaunted men in blue,
A crisis now affairs are coming to.

(*Enter Police from R. I. E., marching in single file.*)

SERGEANT. Though in body and in mind, tarantara! tarantara!
We are timidly inclined, tarantara!
And anything but blind, tarantara! tarantara!
To the danger that's behind, tarantara!
Yet, when the danger's near, tarantara! tarantara!
We manage to appear, tarantara!
As insensible to fear,
As anybody here, tarantara!
Tarantara! tarantara-ra-ra-ra-ra!

MABEL. Sergeant, approach. Young Frederic was to have led you to death and glory.

ALL. That is not a pleasant way of putting it.

MABEL. No matter. He will not so lead you, for he has allied himself once more with his old associates.

ALL. He has acted shamefully!

MABEL. You speak falsely; you know nothing about it. He has acted nobly!

ALL. He has acted nobly!

MABEL. Dearly as I loved him before, his heroic sacrifice to his sense of duty has endeared him to me tenfold; but if it was *his* duty to constitute himself my foe, it is likewise *my* duty to regard him in that light. He has done his duty; I will do mine. Go ye and do yours. (*Exit* MABEL *R. I. E.*)

ALL. Very well.

SERGEANT. This is perplexing.

ALL. We cannot understand it at all.

SERGEANT. Still, if he is actuated by a sense of duty—

ALL. That makes a difference, of course. At the same time, we repeat we cannot understand it.

SERGEANT. No matter. Our course is clear; we must do our best to capture these pirates alone. It is most distressing to us to be the agents whereby our erring fellow-creatures are deprived of that liberty which is so dear to all, but we should have thought of that before we joined the force.

ALL. We should.

SERGEANT. It is too late now.

ALL. It is.

SONG.—SERGEANT.

When a felon's not engaged in his employment—
ALL. His employment,
SERGEANT. Or maturing his felonious little plans—
ALL. Little plans,
SERGEANT. His capacity for innocent enjoyment—
ALL. -Cent enjoyment

SERGEANT. Is just as great as any honest man's—
ALL. Honest man's.
SERGEANT. Our feelings we with difficulty smother—
ALL. -Culty smother,
SERGEANT. When constabulary duty's to be done—
ALL. To be done.
SERGEANT. Ah, take one consideration with another—
ALL. With another,
SERGEANT. A policeman's lot is not a happy one—
ALL. Happy one.
When constabulary duty's to be done—
To be done—
The policeman's lot is not a happy one—
Happy one!
SERGEANT. When the enterprising burglar's not a-burgling—
ALL. Not a-burgling,
SERGEANT. When the cutthroat isn't occupied in crime—
ALL. -Pied in crime,
SERGEANT. He loves to hear the little brook a-gurgling—
ALL. Brook a-gurgling,
SERGEANT. And listen to the merry village chime—
ALL. Village chime.
SERGEANT. When the coster's finished jumping on his mother—
ALL. On his mother,
SERGEANT. He loves to lie a-basking in the sun—
ALL. In the sun.
SERGEANT. Ah, take one consideration with another—
ALL. With another,
SERGEANT. The policeman's lot is not a happy one—
ALL. Happy one!
When constabulary duty's to be done—
To be done,
The policeman's lot is not a happy one—
Happy one!

CHORUS OF PIRATES OUTSIDE, IN THE DISTANCE.

A rollicking band of pirates we,
Who, tired of tossing on the sea,
Are trying their hand at a burglaree
With weapons grim and gory!

SERG. Hush! hush! I hear them on the manor poaching;
With stealthy step the pirates are approaching.

CHORUS OF PIRATES RESUMED NEARER.

We are not coming for plate or gold—
A story General Stanley told—

We seek a penalty fifty-fold
For General Stanley's story.

POLICE. They seek a penalty.
PIRATES. (*Without.*) Fifty-fold!
We seek a penalty fifty-fold!
ALL. We { seek a penalty fifty-fold
They { for General Stanley's story.
POLICE. They come in force,
With stealthy stride;
Our obvious course
Is now to hide.

(*Police conceal themselves in aisle L. As they do so the Pirates, with* RUTH *and* FREDERIC, *are seen appearing at ruined window C. They enter cautiously, and come down stage on tiptoe. The* KING *is laden with burglarious tools and pistols, etc. etc.*)

CHORUS.—PIRATES.

(*Very loud.*) With cat-like tread
Upon our prey we steal—
In silence dread
Our cautious way we feel.

POLICE. (*Pianissimo.*) Tarantara! tarantara!
PIRATES. No sound at all:
We never speak a word;
A fly's footfall
Would be distinctly heard.
POLICE. Tarantara! tarantara!
PIRATES. Ha! ha!
Ho! ho!
So stealthily the pirate creeps
While all the household soundly sleeps.
Gurr! gurr!
Gurr! gurr! (*Imitating snoring.*)
Ha! ha! Ho! ho!
POLICE. (*Pianissimo.*) Tarantara! Tarantara!
(*Forte.*) Tarantara!
PIRATES. Come friends, who plough the sea,
Truce to navigation;
Take another station;
Let us vary piracy
With a little burglary!
SAMUEL. Here's your crowbar
And your centre-bit;
Your life-preserver—
You may want to hit!

Your silent matches,
Your dark-lantern seize;
Take your file and your skeleton keys!

PIRATES. With catlike tread, etc.

POLICE. Tarantara, tarantara, etc.

RECIT.—FRED.

Hush! not a word! I see a light inside.

(*Looks through keyhole L.*)

The major-general comes, so quickly hide.

MAJOR-GENERAL. (*Without.*) Yes, yes, the major-general comes.

PIRATES. He comes!

MAJOR-GENERAL. (*Entering in dressing-gown, carrying a light.*) Yes, yes, I come!

POLICE. He comes!

MAJOR-GENERAL. Yes, yes, I come.

ALL. The major-general comes!

SOLO.—GENERAL.

Tormented with the anguish dread
Of falsehood unatoned,
I lay upon my sleepless bed,
And tossed and turned and groaned.
The man who finds his conscience ache
No peace at all enjoys;
And as I lay in bed awake
I thought I heard a noise.

PIRATES. He thought he heard a noise!
Ha! ha! ha! ha! ha! ha!

POLICE. He thought he heard a noise!
Tarantara-ra-ra!

GENERAL. No, all is still
In dale, on hill;
My mind is set at ease.
So still the scene
It might have been
The sighing of the breeze.

BALLAD.—GENERAL.

Sighing softly to the river
Comes the lonely breeze,
Setting Nature all a-quiver,
Rustling through the trees.

ALL. Through the trees.

GENERAL. And the brook in rippling measure
Laughs for very love,
While the poplars in their pleasure
Wave their arms above.

POLICE *and* PIRATES. Yes, the trees for very love
Wave their leafy arms above.
River, river, little river!
May thy loving prosper ever!
Heaven speed the poplar tree!
May thy wooing happy be!

GENERAL. Yes, the breeze is but a rover!
When he wings away,
Brook and poplar mourn a lover,
Sighing "Well-a-day!"

ALL. Well-a-day!

GENERAL. Ah, the doing and undoing
That the rogue could tell!
When the breeze is out a-wooing,
Who can woo so well?

POLICE *and* PIRATES. Shocking tales the rogue could tell;
Nobody can woo so well!
Pretty brook, thy dream is over,
For thy love is but a rover.
Sad the lot of poplar trees
Courted by a fickle breeze!

(*Enter the* GENERAL'S *daughters, led by* MABEL, *all in white peignoirs and nightcaps, and carrying candles.*)

GIRLS. Now, what is this? and what is that? and why does father leave his rest
At such a time of night as this, so very incompletely dressed?
Dear father is, and always was, the most methodical of men;
It's his invariable rule to go to bed at half-past ten.
What strange occurrence can it be that calls dear father from his rest
At such a time of night as this, so very, so very incompletely dressed?

KING. (*Springing up.*) Forward, my men, and seize that general there!
His life is over.

GENERAL. The pirates! Oh, despair!

MABEL *and* GIRLS. The pirates! the pirates!
Oh, despair!

PIRATES. Yes, yes, we are the pirates, so despair!

GENERAL. Frederic here? Oh joy! oh rapture!—
Summon your men and effect their capture.

MABEL. Frederic, save us!

FRED. Beautiful Mabel,
I would if I could, but I am not able.
PIRATES. He's telling the truth; he is not able.

(*They seize the* GENERAL.)

KING. With base deceit
You worked upon our feelings;
Revenge is sweet,
And flavors all our dealings.
With courage rare,
And resolution manly,
For death prepare,
Unhappy General Stanley!
FRED. (*Coming forward.*) Alas! alas! unhappy General Stanley!
POLICE. (*Pianissimo.*) Tarantara! tarantara!

(*They bind the* GENERAL *to broken pillar C.*)

MABEL. (*Wildly.*) Is he to die, unshriven and unannealed?
GIRLS. Oh spare him!
MABEL. Will no one in his cause a weapon wield?
GIRLS. Oh spare him!
POLICE. (*Springing up.*) Yes, we are here, though hitherto concealed.
GIRLS. Oh, rapture!
POLICE. So to our powers, pirates, quickly yield!
GIRLS. Oh, rapture!

(*A struggle ensues between Pirates and Police,* RUTH *tackling* SERGEANT. *Eventually the Police are overcome and fall prostrate, the Pirates standing over them with drawn swords.*)

PIRATES.	POLICE.
We triumph now, for well we trow	You triumph now, for well we trow
Your mortal career's cut short;	Our mortal career's cut short;
No pirate band will take its stand	No pirate band will take its stand
At the Central Criminal Court.	At the Central Criminal Court.

GENERAL. To gain a brief advantage you've contrived,
But your proud triumph will not be long-lived!
KING. Don't say you're orphans, for we know that game.
SERGEANT. On your allegiance we've a stronger claim:
We charge you yield, in Queen Victoria's name!
KING. (*Baffled.*) You do?

POLICE. We do!
We charge you yield in Queen Victoria's name!

(*Pirates kneel; Police stand over them triumphantly.*)

KING. We yield at once with humbled mien,
Because, with all our faults, we love our queen.
POLICE. Yes, yes, with all their faults they love their queen.

(*Police, holding Pirates by the collar, take out handkerchiefs and weep.*)

GENERAL. Away with them, and place them at the bar!
RUTH. One moment; let me tell you who they are.
They are no members of the common throng;
They are all noblemen who have gone wrong.
GENERAL, POLICE, *and* GIRLS. What! *All* noblemen?
KING *and* PIRATES. Yes, *all* noblemen!
GENERAL, POLICE, *and* GIRLS. What! All?
KING. Well, nearly all.
GENERAL. No Englishman unmoved that statement hears,
Because, with all our faults, we love our House of Peers!

(*All kneel.*)

RECIT.—GENERAL.

I pray you pardon me, ex-pirate king;
Peers will be peers, and youth will have its fling.
Resume your ranks and legislative duties,
And take my daughters, all of whom are beauties.

(*All rise. Each Pirate takes a Girl.*)

FINALE.

RUTH. At length we are provided, with unusual facility,
To change piratic crime for dignified respectability.
KING. Combined, I needn't say, with the unparalleled felicity
Of what we have been longing for—unbounded domesticity.
MABEL. To-morrow morning early we will quickly be parsonified—
Hymeneally coupled, conjugally matrimonified.
SERGEANT. And this shall be accomplished by that doctor of divinity
Who happily resides in the immediate vicinity.
CHORUS. Who happily resides in the immediate vicinity.

GENERAL. My military knowledge, though I'm plucky and adventury,
Has only been brought down to the beginning of the century;
But still, in getting off my daughters—eight or nine or ten in all—
I've shown myself the model of a modern major-general,

ALL. His military knowledge, etc.

(*Dance.*)

CURTAIN.

THE END.